Adult Coloring Book
Fanciful Fashions

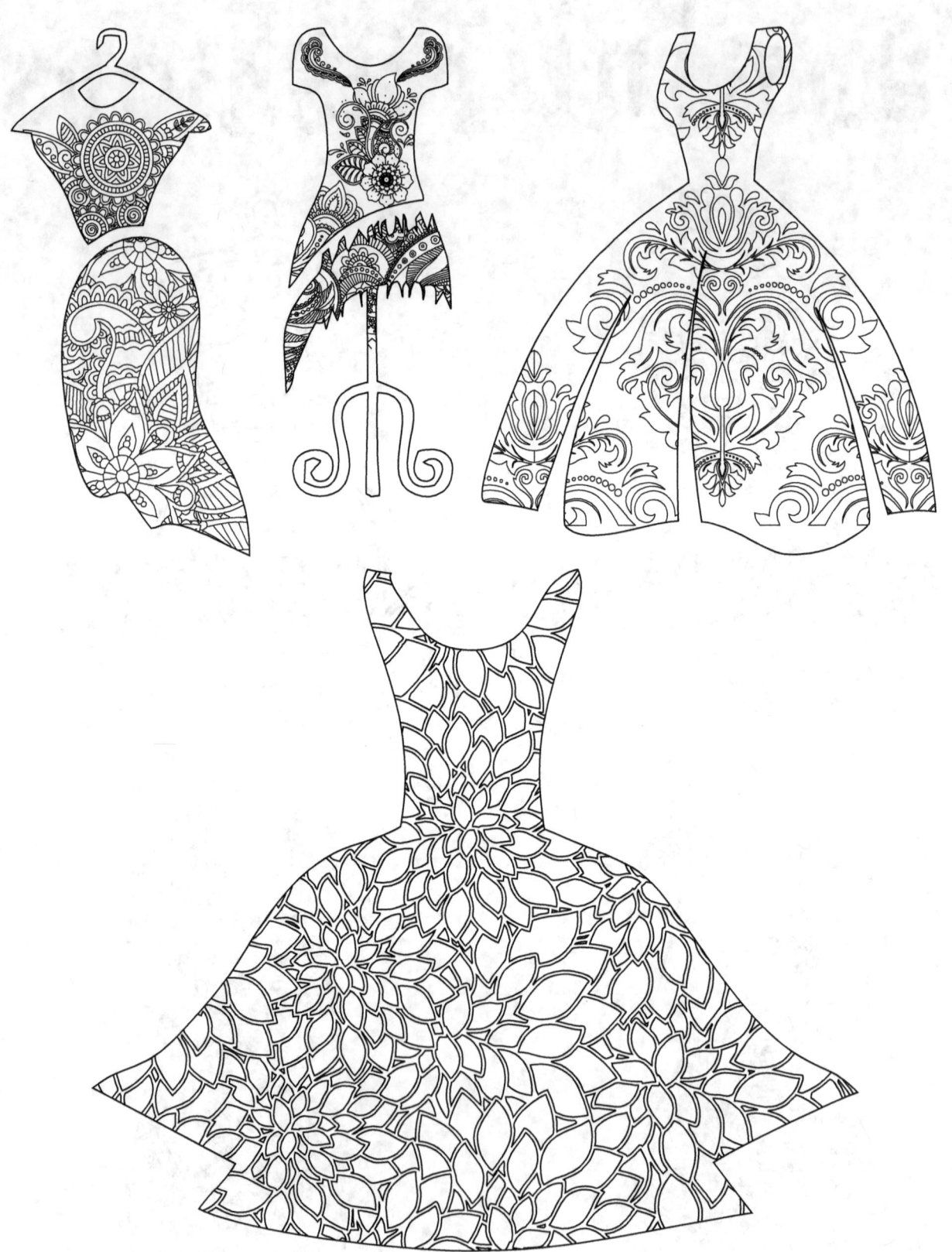

Adult Coloring Book
Fanciful Fashions

By Alpa Rationalist

Published by
Eagle Eye Enterprise

Copyright Notice

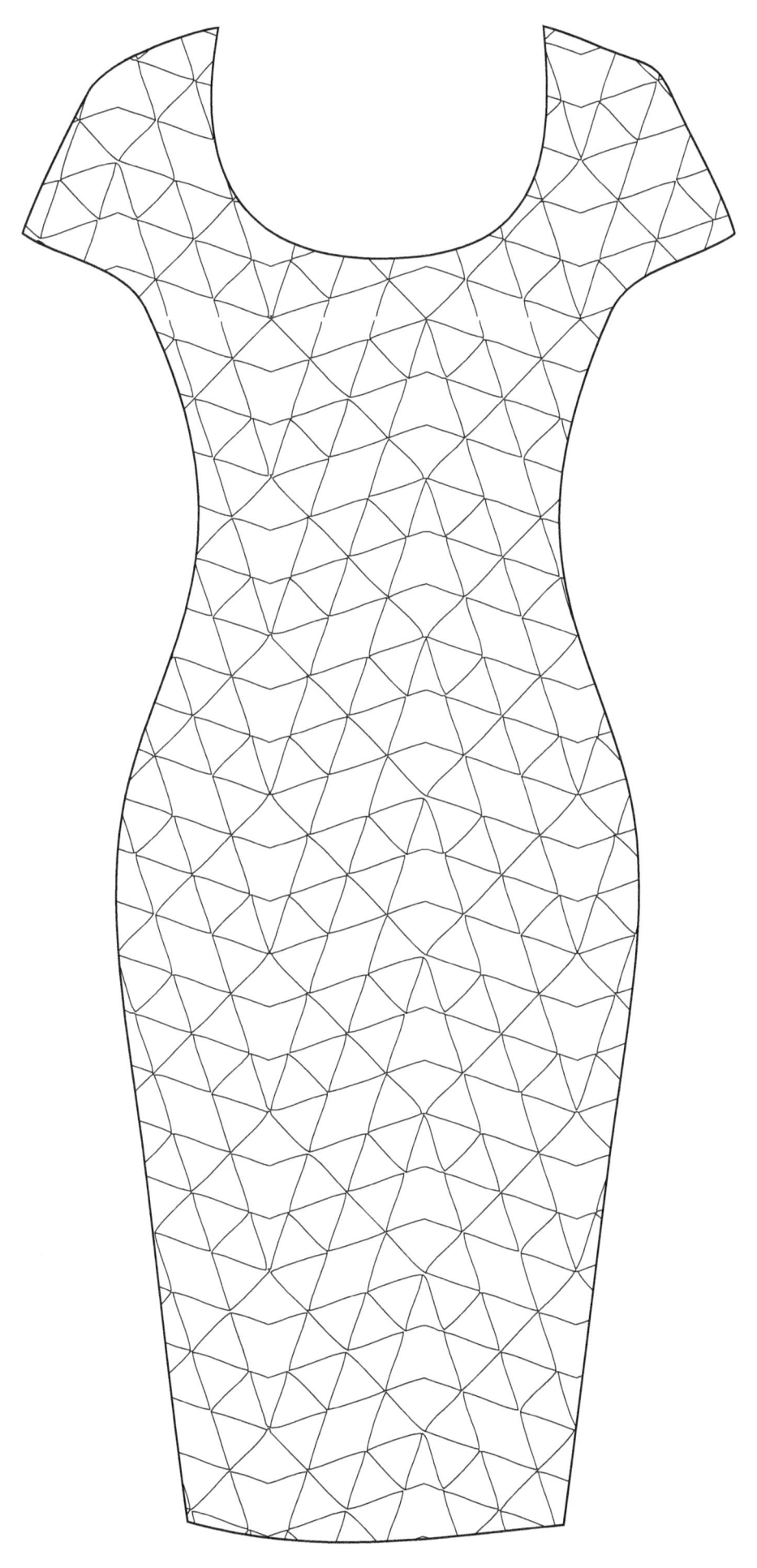

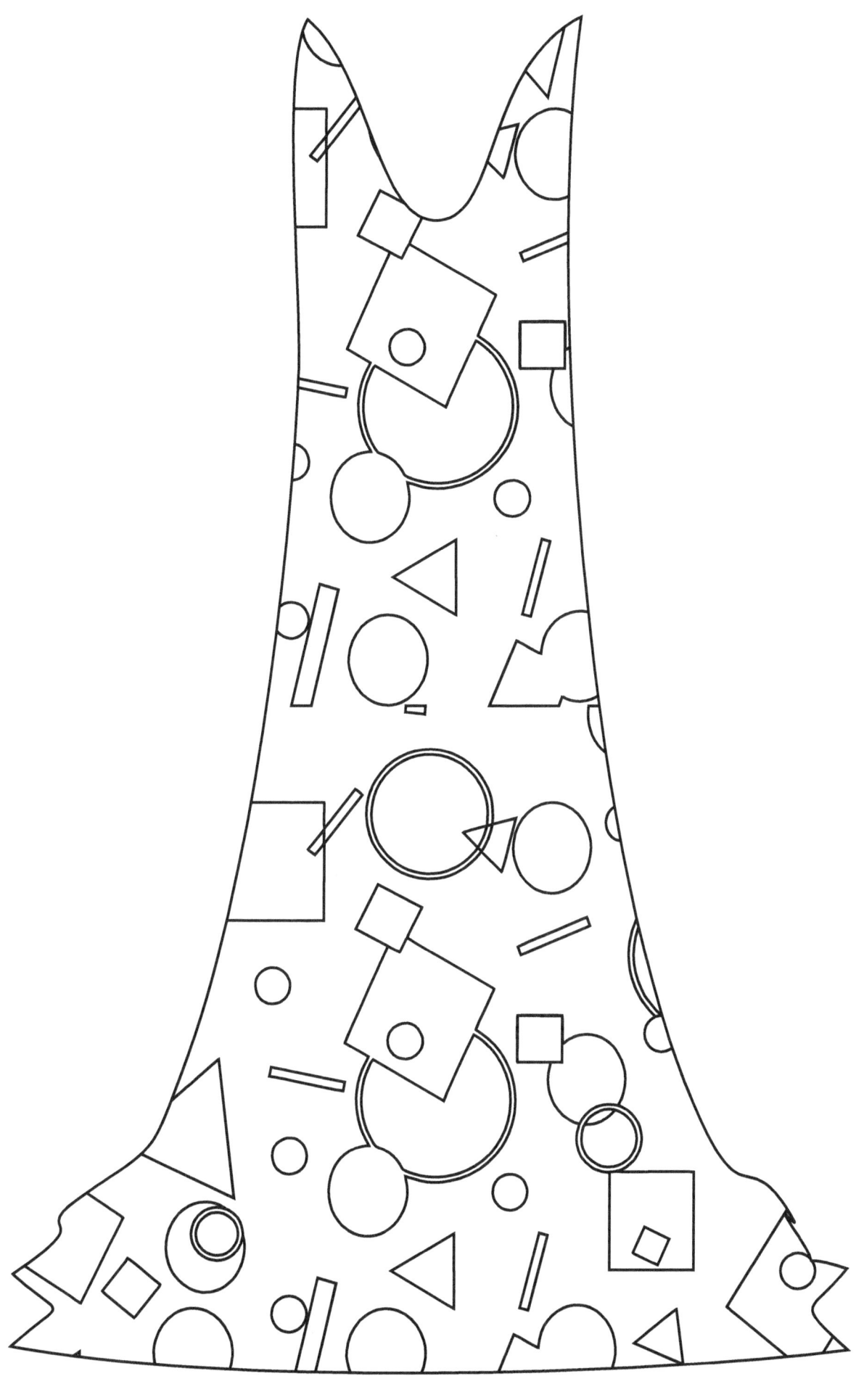

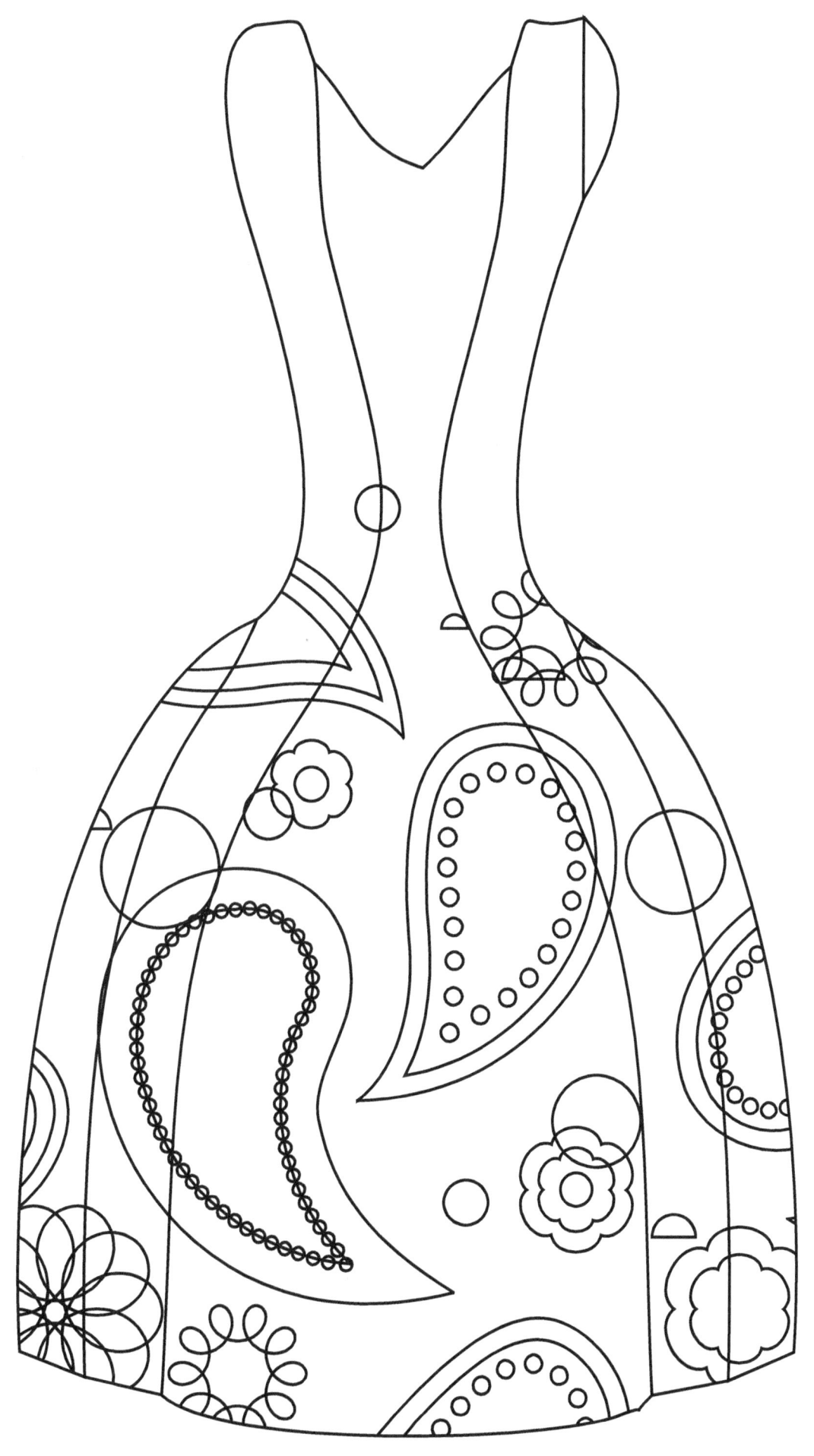

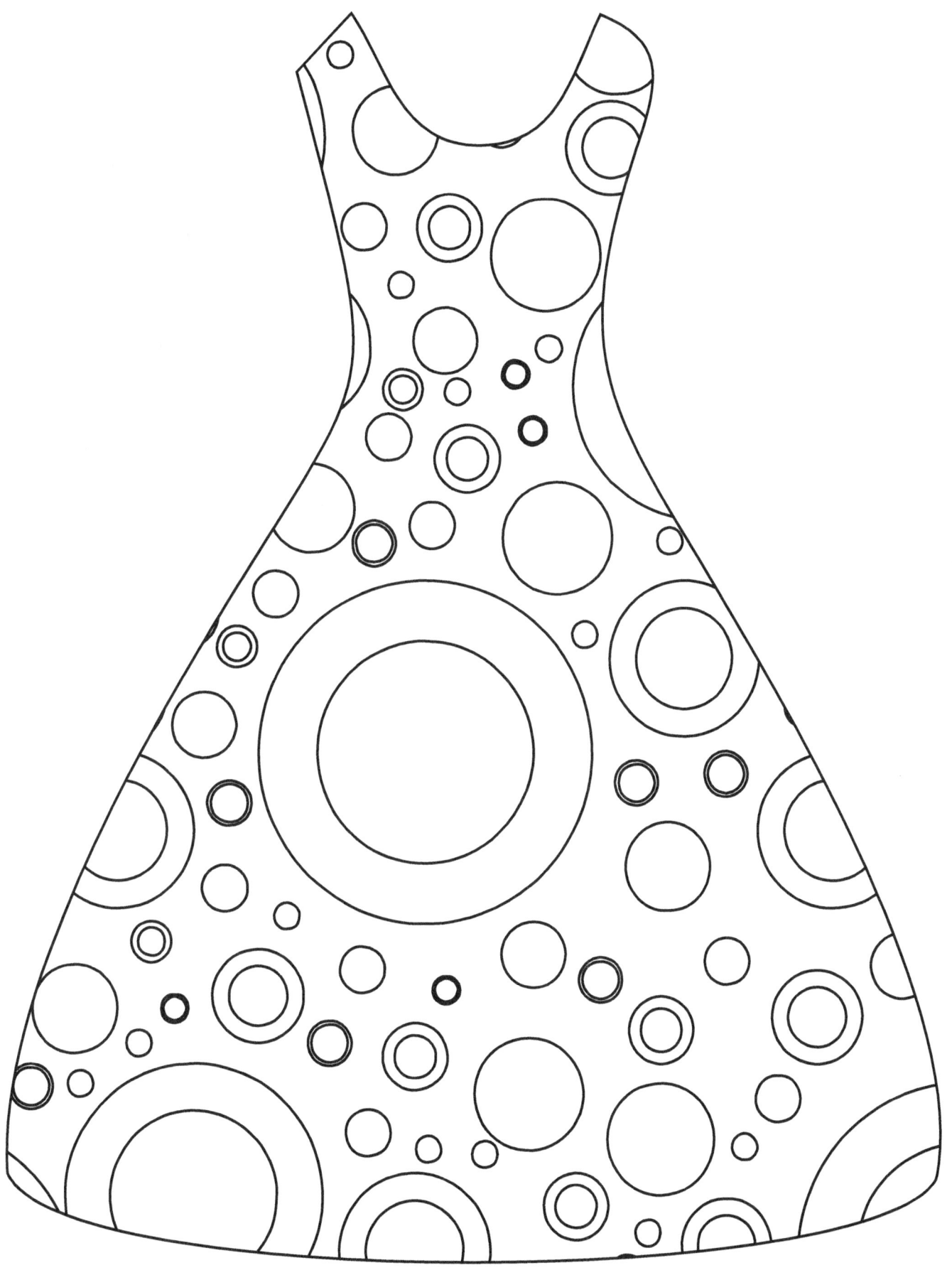

www.ingramcontent.com/pod-product-compliance
Lightning Source LLC
Chambersburg PA
CBHW080440290526
45791CB00008BA/2561